Experien

A Practioner's Guide To Integrating Appreciative Inquiry With Experiential Learning

by
Miriam Ricketts
and
James Willis
Executive Edge, Inc.

Taos Institute

EXPERIENCE AI

Other Taos Focus Books:
Appreciative Leaders: In the Eye of the Beholder. (2001) Edited by Marjorie Schiller,
    Bea Mah Holland, and Deanna Riley
The Appreciative Organization. (2001) Harlene Anderson, David Cooperrider, et. al.

FIRST EDITION
Copyright © 2001 by
Miriam Ricketts & Jim Willis

ISBN 0-9712312-2-2   PRINTED IN U.S.A.

Our Thanks

First and foremost, we would like to thank our friends and family, including our Executive Edge family — Elissa Katz, Jason Klein, Molly McGuigan, Rhoda Reyzman, and Audrey Shilling — for not only putting up with us while writing this book, but also for their support and encouragement, and for helping us to keep things on track in our personal and professional lives.

Thanks also to our colleagues and clients, whose ideas and enthusiasm helped inspire the concepts and experiences included in this book: Dawn Dole (probably the most appreciative person we know), David Cooperrider, Gerri Hura and her staff at the Baldwin Wallace College Professional Development Center, Professor Sandy Maltby and her Entrepreneurship students, Juli Lynch, Fred Goodnow, Leslie Yerkes, Dave Tierno, Jackie Kelm, Ellen Glazerman, Robert Means, Chris Schenk, Laura Smith Nolte, Catherine Graham and Rudolf Arend. Thank you for challenging and inspiring us!

A very special thank you to Ken Gergen for inviting us, without a moment's hesitation, to write this book and Jane Seiling for her absolutely unwavering generosity, wisdom and competence. You both inspire us.

1 Introduction

Appreciative Inquiry (AI) is a transformational organization change process. People experiencing an AI inspire each other to leverage their most powerful collective stories in order to dream and design a new affirmative future. In the process of truly hearing each other's hopes and dreams, people create community — they discover affinity, build relationships, and develop common language with those who were previously only colleagues in the most formal sense. AI at its best generates an energy that causes people to change rapidly and positively in relation to each other and in doing so their organizations and communities are transformed to the extent that they are never again the same.

Now, what if, in conjunction with telling stories about encounters with excellence and while sharing aspirations, people could also experience excellence and make their dreams come alive, in real time? What if the AI process could shift from thinking to doing, from the cerebral domain to the kinesthetic, from storytelling to experiencing — where dreams from the imagination about working well together immediately manifest into physical experience?

Imagine an AI into the topic of "how exemplary leadership happens" where company leaders practice living their Provocative Propositions (those powerful affirmative statements that inspire a group toward its ideal future) in a compressed time micro-world

— a complex outdoor orienteering course. Or, imagine an Enterprise Resource Planning (ERP) software installation process spearheaded by two heavily siloed departments (Finance & Information Technology Services). While holding each other's safety ropes, team members scale a 50-foot scaffolding structure to cross-train each other in their subject matter areas, creating a horizontal process that connects and leads the organization toward achieving a common collaborative goal. Or, using a different kind of experience, imagine an Appreciative Inquiry into the topic of "inspirational leadership" where the leadership potential of an organization's key executives is activated by a community service challenge, specifically feeding and clothing 2,000 people in 24 hours.

Imagine there are moments during these experiences when everyone "gets it," the synergy flows and collective dreams come to life. How would such "group peak experiences" enable an organization's ability to create and accelerate sustainable and systemic change?

We deeply believe in the power of Experiential Learning (EL), a formalized process for reflecting on experience in order to extract meaningful learning and to develop tacit knowledge. By sharing and learning from common experience, people attain the high levels of rapport, empathy, trust and mutual understanding necessary to risk and embrace change together. When integrated into each stage of an Appreciative Inquiry, Experiential Learning supports and illuminates the AI process, making each phase "come alive" for all stakeholders.

Why read this book

Experience AI: A Practitioner's Guide To Integrating Appreciative Inquiry With Experiential Learning is valuable for anyone engaged in an individual, team or organizational change process. It is written with the intent of starting a conversation around the power and efficacy of embedding Experiential Learning models, tools and techniques into Appreciative Inquiry — in order to accelerate positive change, motivate teams and individuals, generate buy-in and engage people at all levels. If you believe that accelerating learning and change cycle times is just as important as reducing product cycle times, you should read this book.

About Us

Our corporate consulting practice, Executive Edge, Inc. was founded in 1989, and is rooted in the fields of experiential, classroom and wilderness education, expeditioning, international business and organization development. Throughout the years, we have kept one foot in the natural world, which has helped us to become better consultants. Our combined life experiences (and observation of human interactions in wild places) have helped us to see natural patterns and rhythms in organizations, and to create learning experiences that are fundamentally different from most corporate learning programs.

Unique Components

The following is a brief overview of several unique components of this integrated process. These components will be explored and applied to the client scenarios throughout the book.

Self-Facilitated Team Learning™

Over the years, through study and a good bit of trial and error, we have discovered several components that heighten the impact of EL for the adult learner. *These learnings help to successfully merge EL with AI.* The most significant of these is what we call Self-Facilitated Team Learning, a process that guides group learning while placing the responsibility for facilitation almost entirely into the hands of the participants. Groups learn how to facilitate a process for extracting meaningful learning from experience while reaching toward the goal of continuous improvement. Not only do they move from a state of dependence to independence (from the external facilitator). Through self-facilitation they develop a sense of interdependence within their team or participant group. The external facilitator is thus freed to elevate learning to another level.

Due to its learner-centered focus, Self-Facilitated Team Learning is especially effective in compressed time situations (in which learning cycle times are drastically cut).

Continuous Learning Cycle™

The Continuous Learning Cycle is the heart of Self-Facilitated Team Learning. This model enables a group or team to extract meaningful learning from experience and immediately apply it using an action, reflection, analysis, strategy and application process. (See model on page 14.)

Team Learning Journals™

Participants guide their learning by using a detailed "learning map" called the Team Learning Journal. Team Learning Journals contain everything the participants need to conduct their own activities and facilitate their own learning processes — activity frontloading, scenarios, rules and reflective debrief tools. Self-facilitating groups use Team Learning Journals to help manage their time, call their own process breaks ("time-out" from the task for the group to reevaluate strategy, group dynamics etc.), prioritize the value of each activity, and conduct their own debriefs.

Integrated Program Flow

One of the most important concepts introduced in this book explains the way in which program flow makes for a truly integrated approach. An integrated AI/EL process flows as a traditional AI would — participants travel the 4-D Cycle (developed by David Cooperrider and colleagues at Case Western Reserve University in Cleveland, OH). Integrated into the flow with the 4-D Cycle are two other processes: The Relationship Continuum™ (a model for relationship development, see chart on page 29) and The Continuous Learning Cycle (a model for extracting meaningful learning from experience). The interplay of all three processes is the key to creating powerful, accelerated learning experiences.

A Look At What's Ahead

In **Chapter Two:** Telling the Tale and Living It dives more deeply into AI and EL, looking at the effectiveness of integrating

EL into each stage of the AI 4-D cycle: Discovery, Dream, Design and Destiny. **Chapters Three through Six** introduce four client stories that highlight how the integrated experiential components maximize learning.

- **Chapter Three:** Discovery — The NYC Leadership Challenge
- **Chapter Four:** Dream — A Call to Collaborative Action
- **Chapter Five:** Design — Exemplary Team Leadership
- **Chapter Six:** Destiny — Project Success

Chapter Seven: Self-Facilitated Team Learning — Reinventing Experiential Learning and Re-defining the Facilitator's Role looks at our metamorphosis as Experiential Learning consultants, and gives a more detailed look at current shifts in the field of Experiential Learning. **Chapter Eight:** The Beginning reviews how Experiential Learning supports basic AI principles, and summarizes the main concepts discussed throughout the book. There is also a Glossary of Terms in the back of the book that defines unfamiliar or unique words and phrases.

Throughout this Focus Book, we invite you to explore the possibilities for integrating Experiential Learning into the Appreciative Inquiry process. It is our hope that you will see how Experiential Learning contributes to the flow toward mutual understanding that is necessary for people, organizations and communities to discover and live their destiny.

2 Telling the Tale And Living It

Great storytellers recognize that the best stories are a balancing act between fact and fiction, real life and dreams, description and embellishment. These storytellers build rapport with their audience by providing openings so that the readers and listeners can insert their own emotions, experiences, hopes and dreams into the story. The audience becomes engaged in the story because they have developed an experiential and empathic frame of reference based on contributing personal experience and emotion to the plot. They are invited to "live" within the story, to make their own stories come alive within the context of the tale.

The traditional Appreciative Inquiry (AI) 4-D approach engages people in much the same way. First, it introduces the potential for a new, compelling, and generative future. It proceeds by asking people to tell stories about their personal experiences with success, and to relate these stories to their dreams for an affirmative future. Through this process AI inspires people to share their emotions, experiences, hopes and dreams to reinvent and build a new more positive reality. Appreciative Inquiry, in large part due to its storytelling aspects, is very powerful.

Our experience over the past several years is that the AI process can be accelerated, deepened and intensified by integrating structured experiences combined with guided reflective processes (commonly called "Experiential Learning" [EL]) that are imbued with the AI philosophy and embedded into the AI 4-D Cycle.

Experiential Learning that is skillfully integrated into an Appreciative Inquiry literally makes the entire AI process come alive. EL accelerates learning, relationship building and change processes. In addition, EL rapidly develops rapport, builds empathy, deepens trust and heightens mutual understanding among all stakeholders. When designed into an AI process, EL:

- Impels people into **actually experiencing** "the best of what exists" (Discovery)
- Creates common language and shared empathy (Discovery, Dream)
- Brings collective dreams and aspirations to life (Dream)
- Creates opportunities for organizational "peak experiences" — real time moments when the entire stakeholder group "lives" its dreams (Discovery, Dream)
- Enhances data collection, adding to the quantity and quality of collected data (Discovery, Dream)
- Transcends cultural inhibitions against "prideful speech" and "fanciful thinking" (Discovery, Dream)
- Provides opportunities to experience, practice and refine provocative propositions and principles of practice — generating immediate feedback on their utility and effectiveness (Design)
- Creates learning environments to thaw and reshape communal understanding, language and behaviors (Design, Destiny)
- Builds critical mass as change is cascaded throughout the community (Design, Destiny)
- Helps the AI process to "come alive" kinesthetically, creating "muscle memories" of affirmative communal futures (Discovery, Dream, Design, Destiny)

As a result of participating in shared common experiences and taking risks together in safe, micro-world environments, AI participants may be more likely to take risks together in real life — a necessary step toward re-inventing self and community[1].

What is Experiential Learning?

The roots of Experiential Learning are based in the works of Aristotle and Plato, John Dewey, William James, Kurt Hahn and David Kolb, among others, who have examined ways to extract meaningful learning from experience. Broadly speaking, EL involves an immersion into a structured experience or a series of experiences, combined with meaningful reflection.

The structured experiences that we have integrated with AI run the gamut from team initiatives and "solution-finding" activities to business simulations, the performing arts, Service Learning and Action Learning. The experiences are integrated with facilitated and/or self-facilitated reflective processes that help the learners explore what happened during the experience, analyze the patterns that emerged, strategize for the next experience and transfer learning to another environment (work, home, school, etc.).

The key is to discover and extract the most relevant, appropriate and, therefore, the most meaningful learning. There is a short story by Mark Twain that is commonly referenced in the EL community about a cat who sits on a hot stove. Rumor has it (because we have never actually witnessed this) that the cat will never sit on a hot stove again. It will also never sit on a cold stove, because it did not extract all of the learning that it might have from its experience.

The Continuous Learning Cycle

The Continuous Learning Cycle model (refined from David Kolb's Experiential Learning Cycle[2]) is a powerful tool for maximizing learning. The model begins with a concrete experience that is framed to mirror the client's culture, business models and learning objectives. After completing the experience, the learner follows a "What? So What? Now What?" questioning process that guides the learner through reflection, inquiry and transference of learning from the experience.

The CLC is also supported by a foundation of three learning dimensions — Content, Context and Community[3]. The CLC model not only elicits learning *content* (e.g. collaborative teaming), but it also highlights the *context* in which work takes place (e.g. multiple teams collaborating together in order to achieve a common goal)

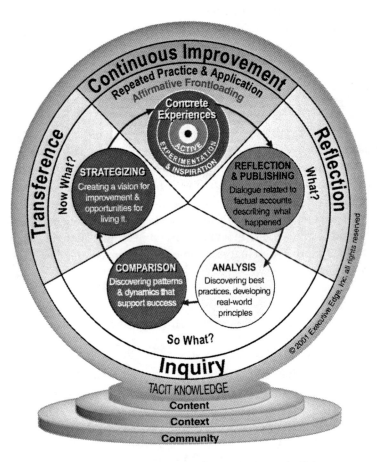

Continuous Learning Cycle Model maximizing appropriate learning from concrete experience

and the *community* within which work is performed (e.g. collaborative teaming in a community of engineers). The interaction between the CLC and the "Three C's" creates opportunities for discovery, exploration, experimentation, practice and application, strategizing and improvement.

EL is one of the most effective methods of adult learning for developing tacit knowledge needed by a person or group in order to perform in the workplace. Vis-à-vis traditional learning (where content is delivered through lectures or presentations), Experiential Learning is participative. It takes place in purposefully constructed "micro-worlds"[4] (or experiential learning laboratories) in which content is delivered and potentials are discovered while the learners are immersed within the context and community in which the learning will be applied.

While within the "micro-world," participants encounter structured learning experiences in which behaviors, interpersonal relationships, interactions and decision-making styles are mirrored back in the form of recognizable patterns and dynamics. In micro-worlds that accurately reflect workplace settings, people learn together by conducting experiments that they would rarely attempt to conduct in the real workplace community.

A Brief Look at Traditional AI

Traditional Appreciative Inquiry (AI)[5], is based on four steps (the AI 4-D Cycle) — Discovery (D^1), Dream (D^2), Design (D^3) & Destiny (D^4). The appreciative process begins by asking people to tell stories about their experiences with success and to relate these stories to their dreams for the future. The storytelling captures individual experiences and aspirations in order to build and reinvent community.

Discovery (D^1)

Discovery (D^1) in the AI sense is learning from and building on personal and group experiences through storytelling. Through Discovery we provide a basis for sharing the best of ourselves in order to build community. Discovery opens up lines of communication and creates opportunities for honest dialogue to take place. In its simplest terms, Discovery is developing rapport.

Discovery (D¹) and EL

In theory, Discovery and Dream are separate processes. In practice, we find that they frequently occur concurrently.

According to Abraham Maslow, peak experiences are addictive — once someone has had a peak experience, they realize new possibilities and they make every attempt to recreate the circumstances around which it occurred, in order to make the experience happen again. Our experience shows that this is as true for groups as it is for individuals. The trick with EL is to connect the peak experience to the desired learning outcomes.

In Discovery, when combining EL with AI, not only are stories of excellence extracted from generative interviews, those stories are manifested into "peak moments of excellence" through structured physical experiences and interpersonal interaction. The participants invoke and apply the "best of their past and present" in a real, physical micro-world environment.

Through Discovery people build emotional bonds and friendly relationships based on mutual liking, trust, and a sense that they understand and share each other's experiences and concerns. By participating in Discovery people develop rapport, eliciting tales of collective experiences with excellence that lead to building positive energy, relationships and community. By developing rapport, Discovery becomes inspirational, uniting everyone through a shared understanding of experiences and the words and images that describe them. In order for the Discovery process to be rich, profound and successful it is necessary to develop rapport before, during and after the process.

Rapport is an important foundational outcome of the Discovery process because success during the rest of the 4-D Cycle is based on it. Rapport can be quickly developed by using structured experiences combined with storytelling and sharing.

Dream (D²)

Dreaming (D²) in AI supports participants in creating a collective vision of a new future. In the Dream phase people build on the rapport that is developed in Discovery and share their aspirations based on their experiences. Through "dreaming" people identify and understand their collective hopes and aspirations for the future, generating empathy among individuals and within the community.

Empathy is necessary in order for people to be able to share their dreams and to understand and relate to the dreams of others. Again, developing rapport and building empathy are necessary steps for successfully navigating the first two phases of an AI. And by establishing rapport and building empathy, the high level of trust required for success in Design (D^3) naturally occurs.

Dream (D^2) and EL

When integrating EL into the Dream phase, opportunities are created for communal "peak experiences" — short periods of time during which individual and group dreams and aspirations come to tangible life. Through peak experiences the community lives the "best of what could be" in a real-time metaphoric context. Communal peak experiences provide a mental image, a group snapshot if you will, that serves first to illustrate the ideal future and second to provide an easily remembered "photograph" for post-program inspiration.

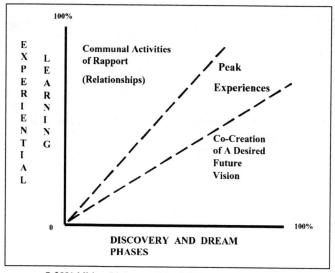

17

Design (D³)

Throughout this process people's understanding of their own identity, their contributions and their standing within the workplace or community shift, sometimes dramatically, to accommodate a new future. People literally reinvent themselves and the systems, processes and structures of their community to fit a new contextual framework — they not only see themselves differently, but the community sees and treats them differently as well. During Design the community can generate working agreements that help to guide and reinforce new concepts and contexts, making it possible to lead, coach and reward members for living in the new way.

Design (D³) can be a sticking point in AI processes. In Design people challenge the status quo, they reinvent themselves, their work and their community in the context of achieving a new future together. In Design individuals and organizations gain the traction necessary to generate sustainable, systemic change. Through provocative propositions they identify and redefine the cultural underpinnings that describe their experiences at work or in their communities. Words like "power," "membership," "representation" and "wealth" are redefined to take on new meaning, expanding a community's capacity for continually moving toward its desired future.

Design (D³) and EL

EL, when merged into Design, provides opportunities for experimenting with and testing provocative propositions and principles of practice in a safe, low-risk environment. Through EL it is possible to create circumstances in which the fruits of Design are put into practice. Design, in this sense, occurs in a micro-world where individual and communal reactions are observed, learning takes place, ideas and images are tested and adjustments are made. Most importantly, groups develop confidence — all in an environment where the negative consequences of making mistakes are minimal.

It is difficult, risky work to re-conceive and reinvent oneself, one's work and one's community. But, there is no doubt that reinvention of self and community is powerful and it is a

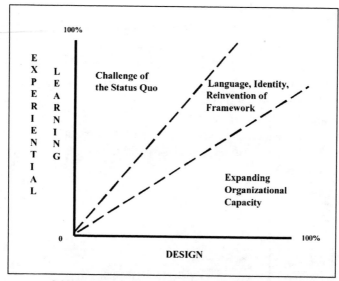

worthy endeavor. It is deep and profound work that not only requires rapport and empathy, but also calls for and builds high levels of interpersonal and communal trust.

Destiny (D⁴)

Destiny provides the opportunity to "live the design." Living the design through acknowledging and acting on one's destiny is living the community's new story with integrity. It no longer feels so risky to live the imagined future.

Success in the Destiny (D^4) phase of the AI 4-D Cycle means giving integrity to the communal vision through one's speech, actions, attitudes and behaviors and utilizing and generating organizational enablers (people, systems, processes and structures) that are aligned with and support the future. Peak experiences, reinvention and mutually living the story come alive through new experiences of integrity and alignment. Integrity, in this context, is guided by mutual understanding that flows from the rapport, empathy and trust experienced together as a community during the first three phases of an Appreciative Inquiry.

Destiny (D⁴) and EL

Again EL provides a means for accelerating and deepening Destiny. Through EL micro-worlds, Destiny can be affirmed and cascaded out to the rest of the community (i.e. those members who were not part of the AI, all new hires as part of their orientation, specific groups to build their momentum for change, etc.), thereby building the critical mass needed in order for lasting change to occur. This ensures that the call for the new communal vision will be understood and, therefore, take root in the minds and hearts of the community.

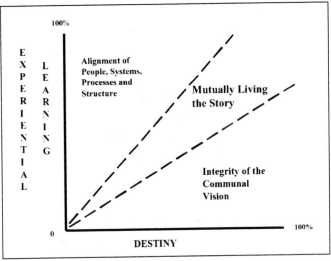

Summary

Through heightened rapport, the community gains the open, honest communication that is essential for successful discovery. Communal empathy creates deep understanding and commitment for supporting the dreams, goals and aspirations of all stakeholders. Trust building makes it possible to continually reinvent one's self and the community while generating new systems and processes that support and are aligned with the desired future. This entire relationship-building process encourages a flow toward the

20

mutual understanding that is necessary for community members to support the future and live their destiny with integrity.

Experiential learning contributes to this process by creating highly interactive and collaborative environments in which current excellence and future dreams can be expressed and realized in compressed time micro-worlds that reflect, and even re-shape, the real world. High levels of interpersonal trust are built and confidence in solutions is established through experimentation, application and practice. As communal understanding increases, solutions are enabled throughout the organization as awareness moves from the minds of a few and takes root in the hearts and hands of the many.

The NYC Leadership Challenge
Learning Journal Interview Questions

Thank you very much for agreeing to participate in this interview.

I am seeking stories that describe how people inspire and lead community change. I understand the dire situation that exists in our inner city. It seems as though the need for change is so huge, and the task for improving peoples' lives in our city so daunting, that achieving success appears to be almost impossible.

Yet, people like you continue to have success in improving our community and in inspiring others to do the same. You and others in our community continue to prove through your own examples that one can create opportunities for clothing, feeding, housing and educating the people in our community who are in need.

- Please describe a time when you were part of, or observed, an extraordinary display of inspirational leadership in your community.
  — How did leadership inspire people to participate in changing their community?
- What is important to you personally about leadership?
  — What do you value most about yourself and the people in your community?
- Imagine that the year is 2005: What do you hope will be the result of the community leadership efforts that have taken place in the last 7 years?
  — How have you and others contributed to these outcomes?
  — What are you working on today (November 12, 2005) that will achieve your dreams for the next 7 years?

Interview script for Discovery & Dream
NYC Leadership Challenge

3 Discovery — The New York City Leadership Challenge

Chapter Three features the story of a management consulting firm that wanted to instill core leadership values and skills through an experience with inspirational community service.

Benefits of Integration

Experiential Learning, when integrated into the Discovery (D^1) phase of an Appreciative Inquiry:

- Allows participants to actually experience "the best of what exists"
- Creates common language and shared empathy
- Brings collective dreams and aspirations to life
- Creates opportunities for organizational "peak experiences" — real time moments when the entire stakeholder group "lives" its dreams
- Enhances data collection, adding to the quantity and quality of collected data
- Transcends cultural inhibitions against "prideful speech" and "fanciful thinking"
- Helps the AI process "come alive" kinesthetically for all stakeholders

---

Situation Assessment

The Client Need

This "Big 5" Management Consulting and Accounting Firm had been experiencing rapid growth (adding approximately 45% new employees per year, including executives) for several years. They also had very high (almost 20%) turnover in each of those years. As you might imagine, the Partners at this firm felt they had not been able to "satisfactorily inculcate" the new executives with the core leadership skills and values important to retaining top talent and ultimately the sustained success of their firm.

The leadership in the firm's New York City offices saw senior management as the group who could influence a new direction for the firm by establishing a more positive and inspirational leadership culture. And since the firm held community service as one of its core values, the leadership also wanted an opportunity to validate and call attention to it as an integral component in a leadership learning program.

In 1998, the head of HR for the firm requested a leadership learning experience that included a 24-hour community service challenge for 80 selected managers. He asked that we create a design connecting their business case to a "Leadership Challenge" that was to include a Service Learning experience. The affirmative topic for the 2-day program was: "Creating Leadership that Inspires Positive Community Change." The location: New York City.

The Micro-World Experience — New York City

The "micro-world" experience designed for the New York City Leadership Challenge was to feed and clothe 2,000 people in New York City within 24 hours — all while interviewing the leaders, volunteers, employees and beneficiaries of the service organizations contacted during the challenge. The interview topic was: "Personal experiences with leadership that inspire positive community change." The experience actually represented a challenge to the senior managers to discover "the best leadership that exists," both regarding current capacities and future potentials, and to bring said capacities and potentials to life over a two-day period (one day for the experience and one day to debrief).

The NYC Leadership Challenge began with the Discovery and Dream phases of an AI. During the first few hours on the morning of Day One, the group built rapport and empathy through participating in exercises and conducting interviews with each other. The interviews encouraged them to describe their experiences with extraordinary leadership within their organization, and to express their dreams for themselves as leaders and how, through achieving them, they might actively and positively expand their impact on the future of the firm.

In teams of 8-10, the senior managers were then given three tasks:

1. Feed and clothe 2000 people in need in NYC within the next 24 hours
2. Interview community stakeholders — community service organization leaders, volunteers, workers, and recipients (primarily the homeless) about their personal experiences with "Leadership that Inspires Positive Change;" and
3. Follow and complete the Self-Facilitated Team Learning Journals (designed to guide learning for remote teams) at the designated time milestones during the challenge.

Each group was accompanied by at least one facilitator from our firm and one from the client. The only constraints were that they were not allowed to mention the challenge, the name of their firm or Executive Edge to outsiders with whom they came in contact.

A Mutiny

At this introductory point, we realized that the challenge was going to work and would be transformational. For many of the participants, the initial response to the challenge was fear, concern and outright refusal. We had a totally unexpected mutiny on our hands! Several of the participants argued that this was an unsafe, and even unethical activity (to ask employees to perform community service as part of a work training exercise). Many, naturally, were also concerned about traveling to areas of the city they had been told to avoid all of their lives.

As the discussion progressed, leaders emerged who argued both sides — to pursue the challenge and to protest the challenge. Finally, they asked all facilitators and Partners to leave the room so they could speak openly and candidly among themselves. Many of the protesters were uncomfortable openly expressing their concerns in front of their bosses. They also perceived ulterior motives in the people who were on the side of proceeding with the challenge — namely, "You are only saying this in order to get promoted. If the Partners weren't in the room I think you would take a different line."

Look What Can Happen in 45 Minutes

To this day we don't know what was said in the room during the 45 minutes that we were gone. However, we can tell you what we saw when they invited the facilitators and Partners to return to the room.

The tenor in the room had changed entirely. The internal stress was almost entirely gone. New leaders had emerged and were being supported by the earlier leaders and the rest of the group:

- The group had split up into separate teams whose purpose was to explore various opportunities for accomplishing the challenge.
- Each group had been established based on personal interests, concerns and core values.
- Empathy for one another had prevailed over personal interests.
- It was obvious that interpersonal rapport had been established.

By our estimation, the goals of the Discovery phase had already been accomplished. Even before the challenge had begun, the experience caused the "best existing leadership qualities" to emerge, to be acknowledged and to be utilized. The entire group exhibited incredible capacity for personal and group leadership. By carefully considering the concerns, values and goals of each person, along with the potential benefits of proceeding with the challenge, the participants chose the best course of action for satisfying individual needs while meeting the objectives of the firm.

26

They had created a compressed time learning experience in which everyone had an opportunity to observe and practice extraordinary leadership. This was truly inspirational!

As the micro-world experience continued, more leadership opportunities confronted the participants. These challenges were met with élan. In order to address individual interests and concerns, the group divided into task teams. Some of their tasks included:

- **Moving goods (clothes, food and medicine) to Honduras** for hurricane relief. Donated goods were jammed up in an inefficient warehousing bottleneck and the Honduran Embassy was having difficulty locating, monitoring and shipping the goods to Honduras. The firm's executives went to the Honduran Embassy's warehouse, assessed the problems, created solutions, administered them and left the solution framework in place in a way that the warehouse staff could administer successfully.
- **Volunteering** as cooks, dishwashers and servers at the Bowery Mission's soup kitchen.
- **Creating a new foundation**, supported by the firm and run by junior executives, to provide just-in-time resources for community organizations in need. This foundation still exists.
- **Packaging, transporting and delivering** frozen food and clothing from Harvest For Hunger to homeless and impoverished families.
- **Canvassing** neighborhoods, family and friends for clothing and food donations, locating people in need of the donations and distributing the donations to them.

They far exceeded the goal of feeding and clothing 2000 people in less than a day (they all were at home and in bed by midnight).

Debriefing the Micro-World Experience

At the end of the challenge, early morning on Day Two, the participants returned to the meeting room to relate the accounts of their experiences during the Challenge, many of which involved real time leadership moments that they experienced while accomplishing their goals.

27

At first in paired interviews, then in table groups of ten people, and finally reporting out to the entire room, they related their experiences and talked about the leadership strengths that they had discovered within themselves and each other during the Challenge. They told the stories from their interviews, relating some of the extreme emotions that they had experienced. Many of them expressed determination to continue volunteering to provide the firm's services to the agencies with whom they had worked, both to give relief to the agency and to create opportunities for effectively training the firm's employees.

Reaffirmation of Commitment to Leadership Development
During the afternoon, the Director of the firm's Leadership Institute led a conversation that further illustrated the firm's commitment to leadership development and outlined in more detail the core leadership values and expectations in the firm.

Statements of Personal Goals and Action Plans
Each person created a personal goal and action plan for future development in the next six to twelve months based upon what they had learned about inspirational leadership from these experiences and targeted toward developing inspirational leadership skills (Design phase). Each person also wrote their goals and milestones into a personal performance contract for the next year, to be reviewed by their mentor (Destiny phase) and to be included in their annual performance review.

Continued Learning
To close the program, and as a follow up for continued learning, the firm sponsored a Habitat for Humanity house building project to be completed with their "counseling families" (basically a vertical slice of the organization with one top executive as mentor, junior executives as coaches and managers and staff as counselees) as a means for cascading the lessons throughout the organization. The Habitat House was finished on schedule, and the firm continues to sponsor Habitat for Humanity homes for those employees who wish to volunteer.

Program Flow and Activity Sequence

Throughout the program we used a design flow and sequence of challenges described in the chart below. The column on the left reflects the AI 4-D Cycle, the middle column reflects the desired outcomes of the Relationship Continuum and the column on the right shows the challenges that the teams faced at each point in the program.

Frontloading & Debrief Focus		Selected Structured Experiences with Continuous Learning Cycle Accelerate Relationships, Learning & Change
4-D Cycle	Relationship Continuum	
Discovery Dream	Rapport ====== Empathy	• Power Walk • Peer Leadership Interviews • Announce Leadership Challenge
Design	Trust	• Self-Organized Teaming • 24 Hour Leadership Challenge • Community Service • Community Leadership Interviews • One-On-One and Group "Publishing" of Personal Leadership Experiences • Redefine Leadership
Destiny	Mutual Understanding	• Personal Commitments to Goals and Milestones • Habitat for Humanity Construction Project

In closing, this case is an excellent example of how integrating AI with EL contributes toward creating a strong Discovery phase for an AI process. The structure of the program flowed from developing rapport and empathy among participants to building trust and mutual understanding. The outcomes with respect to insights into inspirational leadership and the learning transference to workplace performance and retention issues were significant. The next chapter describes an EL program that integrates with the Dream phase of an AI process.

A Call to Collaborative Action
Affirmative Topic Statement

As leaders in our Engineering Services Division, we recognize the power that results from inspiring people and teams toward collaborative action, creating a profound shift in the way that they think and operate, from " ... being individuals who ask, 'What can I create?' to being collaborative people who ask, 'What can we create together?' from thinking and working in isolation to thinking and working together — from the primacy of the parts to the primacy of the whole."[6]

Collaborative action creates a strategic advantage for our company — expanding the capacity of all stakeholders to integrate culture, competencies and processes in order to deliver superior products and services for our customers, greater returns for our investors and enhanced value for our community and workplace.

We see that extraordinary results do not flow exclusively from extraordinary individuals but from creative combinations of extraordinary people who learn how to create new value together.

As leaders we give integrity to our vision for the future by modeling collaborative behaviors, speech, attitudes and thinking and encouraging others to generate new ways of thinking and working together.

Affirmative Topic Introduction for
Engineering Services Division
Area 51: Building Collaborative Relationships

4 Dream
— A Call To Collaborative Action

Chapter Four features the story of an engineering services division of a U.S. based European auto manufacturer who experienced a "peak" collaborative moment from an AI-based "Area 51 Learning Experience™." As is the case with all of the organizations featured in this book, this organization was not in need of "fixing." They merely needed a vehicle for launching themselves out of the status quo and into a new future.

The Benefits of Integration

Experiential Learning, when integrated into the Dream (D^2) phase of an Appreciative Inquiry:

- Creates commonly shared language, empathy and goals
- Brings collective dreams and aspirations to life
- Creates opportunities for organizational "peak experiences" — real time moments when the entire stakeholder group "lives" its dreams
- Transcends cultural inhibitions against "prideful speech" and "fanciful thinking"
- Enhances data collection, adding to the quantity and quality of collected data
- Helps the AI process to "come alive" kinesthetically for all stakeholders

---

Situation Assessment

The Client Need

The client, the Director of Engineering Services (ES) for a U.S. based European automobile manufacturer, had been building collaboration within and among his five departments for three years. When he first came to the U.S., each department had its own way of doing things, with little communication or collaboration taking place across the Division's functional stovepipes. In fact, relationships among the departments ranged from non-existent to tribalism and territoriality. According to their Director, they rarely worked together unless forced.

Taking Action

The expanding role of the ES Division required that the departments collaborate, so the first thing that the client did was to bring all five departments together "under one roof." At the same time he urged everyone in each department to consider their jobs, roles and contributions through the lens of the customer (both internal and external), asking them to look particularly at the value they brought and the ease with which the customer was able to access that value.

Because he believed in efficiency, he re-defined and consolidated roles and positions in order to eliminate waste, create operating efficiencies (with technology-based turnkey solutions) and leverage the best talents of his people. In order to achieve this goal he needed to restructure positions. However, keeping in mind that the division needed to grow to meet its expanded role, he also wanted to retain top talent. Therefore, as jobs were phased out through increasing operating efficiencies, new opportunities were created for displaced employees.

Most of the department managers understood the reasons behind this restructuring. They had been working toward this new vision for almost two years. Because of new efforts to collaborate on a regular basis, they were making good progress in achieving their goals. The people on the floor, however, did not have the same collaborative opportunities. Therefore, they did not see the

34

value of working together. In fact, the division's movement toward greater collaboration actually posed a perceived threat in several instances.

As an example, employee documentation of certain job procedures was very important for improving the Division's operating efficiencies. However, many employees felt that by documenting their work, they would dilute their intellectual value, becoming "obsolete" and soon would be out the door. Obviously, this created significant anxiety within the Division.

The employees needed a picture or image to illustrate an affirmative future for them while redefining the present. They needed to see collaboration in action, experience the benefits, face the risks and live what was defined as — "The Dream: A Call to Collaborative Action."

The task was to create learning opportunities (in five and a half hours) for the participants to have collaborative experiences that reflected the Engineering Services (ES) Division of the future. The ideal outcome was to provide a takeaway "snapshot" of group collaboration as a reminder of the experience. This involved changing individual perceptions and behaviors, redefining those principles of practice that confined the ES to the status quo and cascading this image of a new future throughout the organization.

Due to time constraints (5 1/2 hours is not much time) a lot of the program had to be front-loaded. In consultation with the client, the group's Affirmative Topic Statement and provocative propositions were pre-designed. Fortunately, several months prior the client had accomplished a landmark success toward achieving his goals: He had, for all intents and purposes, held an AI Summit (as described by David Cooperrider and Diana Whitney[7]) during which key department stakeholders presented their accomplishments and best practices from the past year. The opportunity was there to leverage much of the energy and momentum from this previous success.

The Micro-World Experience: Area 51 Learning Experience™
About 80 participants (almost all of the ES Division staff) took part in this collaborative workshop. The participants rotated through

the "Area 51 Learning Experience," a joined set of structured initiatives designed to promote team building in an "out-of-this world" theme.

The Area 51 Learning Experience story line challenged the participants

" … to locate the secret U.S. government base called Area 51 (using map and compass) which, according to UFO-logy, houses extraterrestrial beings and their technology. Upon finding Area 51, cross the heavily guarded and mined perimeter, fight an interplanetary dogfight and then find your way into the surgical bunker. Once inside the bunker, perform surgery on the Extra Terrestrials by conducting an 'Alien Organ Transplant.' Post-operative escape plans for the ET's are carried out when your group escapes the bunker through a conveniently placed wormhole and then builds and launches rockets powerful enough to reach escape velocity."

During the program, each team faced five (5) initiative "challenges" that built on each other, much like a novel's chapters develop a complete plot. Two teams met simultaneously at each challenge, and in order to maximize relationship-building opportunities, new teams were mixed together for each rotation. Sample challenges included The Space Walk™ — a 50' long segmented balance beam upon which team members cross a mined and guarded perimeter into Area 51, and Celestial Express™ — a complex series of pulleys and ropes that move space characters from one planet to another on spaceships.

After the teams finished each challenge (or when the time was up, whichever came first) the participants debriefed their experience in order to understand and learn from "the best of what is," and envision "the best of what could be" in their teams. Moreover, as part of the debriefing process, and to illustrate the benefits of inter-team collaboration, each team identified and listed the "best practices" they developed and used during the challenge. The team then left their best practices for the next team arriving at the challenge to use.

Program Flow and Activity Sequence

One aspect to note about the design is the program flow and activity sequence. The challenges were carefully selected for their potential to accomplish specific outcomes. As well, we wrote the affirmative introduction, frontloading and debrief questions to accomplish specific goals for that portion of the program.

The design flow and sequence of challenges are described in the chart below. The column on the left reflects the AI 4-D Cycle, the middle column reflects the desired outcomes of the Relationship Continuum, and the column on the right shows the challenges that the teams faced during the program.

Frontloading & Debrief Focus		Selected Structured Experiences with Continuous Learning Cycle Accelerate Relationships, Learning & Change
4 -D Cycle	**Relationship Continuum**	
Discovery	Rapport	• Power Walk
	======	• Celestial Express™
Dream	Empathy	• Space Walk™
Design	Trust	• Worm Hole™ • Alien Transplant™
Destiny	Mutual Understanding	• Rocket Launch • Closure
© 2001 Executive Edge, Inc. all rights reserved		

As the table illustrates, the first three challenges were designed specifically to promote *rapport* and build *empathy*. Moreover, the group frontloading and reflection periods for these challenges provided (in the form of affirmative frontloading) and generated (through debriefing) meaningful information for the Discovery and Dream phases of the AI process.

The focus shifted during the next set of challenges. These activities emphasized *trust building,* and encouraged the discussion toward changing the status quo. At this point, the group created principles of practice: group norms, systems and processes that nurtured best practices and enabled the future.

Finally, the culminating activities provided opportunities for applying and testing the principles of practice in a highly collaborative setting. The goal here was to establish and articulate *mutual understanding* (which naturally flows from the previous process) and commitment toward actions, speech and attitudes that align with and support a new *Destiny*.

Debriefing the Micro-World Experience

The client found great value in participating in this adventure. Even though the context (working together collaboratively across teams) still existed within the same community, the unfamiliar fantasy world broke perceptual barriers, *creating an intellectually level playing field* in which everyone had equal opportunity for learning and contributing.

People were amazed by the resulting changes in their perspective and seemed surprised by what they were capable of accomplishing. Most of them lead relatively sedentary and departmentally segregated work lives and were completely out of their element in Area 51. They engaged in physical activities that they were unlikely to participate in within the context of their daily lives, with people whom they normally did not associate.

In meeting the physical and intellectual challenges, the participants were so immersed in the moment that they forgot to be self-conscious. In a culture that traditionally valued concrete thinking and self-effacing behavior, they dropped their social masks and interacted as whole people, relating their successes and expressing their dreams both openly and candidly. They began operating from their "positive core."

The participants found a number of deliverables valuable, including :

- discovering that, as a best practice, they could support each other with "no strings" attached
- redefining their team purpose and membership
- experiencing the value of coaching (and being coached)

- recognized that celebrating each other's success breeds more success
- discovering the power of their own and other people's personal, conscious choice making

The client noted recently that he continues to hear comments like: "People who never would have interacted before are now having meaningful conversations here at work!"

In summary, a fantasy micro-world was created with an underlying design that encouraged participants to reflect on and practice collaborative competencies. The teams were composed of people who hardly spoke at work, engaging in unfamiliar physical activities. Yet, in this environment their success depended upon their ability to cooperate, communicate and collaborate with each other in order to achieve a common goal.

If only for a few hours (or more likely, a few minutes within those hours), participants in the Area 51 Learning Experience lived the dream of becoming a highly collaborative ES Division. Those few moments of peak performance served to catalyze systemic, sustainable change within the organization, creating "constructive memory images" for generating a new future back at work.

The next chapter features a different EL program that emphasizes the Design phase of an AI.

Exemplary Team Leadership
Learning Journal Affirmative Topic Statement

It is our desire to become a goal-centered, action-based leadership team that is a shining example for our employees and our industry.

In achieving our objectives, we must strive to exemplify, support and assume ownership for:
- Collaborative Teamwork
- Open Communication
- Creativity Through Risk-taking
- Proactively Initiating and Implementing New Endeavors
- Owning Cross-functional Responsibilities
- Developing Cross-functional Expertise

Affirmative Topic Statement Team Orienteering:
Exemplary Team Leadership

5 Design
— Exemplary Team Leadership

Chapter Five features the story of a small manufacturing company that reinvented its leadership team. In this case the team had an opportunity to "live" its Provocative Propositions (reflecting a future with Exemplary Team Leadership) in a compressed time micro-world — a complex outdoor orienteering course.

The Benefits of Integration

Experiential Learning, when integrated into the Design (D³) phase of an Appreciative Inquiry:

- Provides opportunities to create, practice and refine provocative propositions and principles of practice — generating immediate feedback on their utility and effectiveness
- Creates learning environments to thaw and reshape communal understanding and behaviors
- Builds critical mass as change is cascaded throughout the community
- Helps the AI process "come alive" kinesthetically for all stakeholders

---

Situation Assessment

The Client Need

Our client, the head of a small Ohio manufacturing company, wanted to shift from a top-down management style to developing a more flattened, collaborative focus that empowered her leadership team to make key decisions throughout the company. Historically, all major business decisions in this family-owned company had been funneled through two executive owners (who had very strong personalities). As both men approached retirement, they agreed to bring in a younger member of the family to run the company. Considering the challenge that she faced in transitioning the organization's leadership, she asked Executive Edge to design a process that would help the team and the organization develop a smooth flow toward a more cross-functional leadership structure.

Although the group had worked together for several years, they had little experience working collaboratively. The leadership team was relatively unaware of individual team member strengths and capabilities. As well, the leadership tended to communicate indirectly and hierarchically — receiving third-hand information that was potentially inaccurate, untimely, anonymous and without ownership. Many team members also seriously questioned whether the outgoing executives would have confidence enough in the new leadership to back away and allow long-term changes to occur in the organization.

The Process

An integrated AI/EL program was proposed for kick-starting Exemplary Team Leadership (8 hours conducted over 2 days). The goal was to lay the foundation for building a more collaborative leadership team, with the intention of creating a model for exemplary leadership and teamwork that could be used throughout the entire organization. Specifically, during the program team members would:

- Explore their "best" current leadership practices
- Identify the tools and skills that each member contributes to the leadership team

- Co-create the ideal collaborative future for their team, and
- Test that future in a real-time micro-world learning environment

Approximately two weeks before the program, each participant received an introductory letter and interview packet that included tips for conducting interviews, an interview script and summary sheets to complete and bring with them on the program day. Their task was to find and interview two people at work about their stories of exemplary workplace leadership and their experiences and hopes for the future of leadership in their organization. Sample interview questions included:

1. I'd like to ask you about one key area that we think is important to our company's future — Exemplary Leadership. Tell a story from your life's experience that illustrates leadership by example.
   - What do you value about the leader in the story?
   - What makes him or her an exemplary leader?
2. Please relate a story from your experience when leadership at our company inspired everyone who works here to achieve their greatest potential.
   - What did our leaders do that inspired you?
   - What did you most respect about how our leaders behaved during this time?
   - What did you value most about how everyone in the company responded?
3. If you could transform our current approach to leadership in any way, what three wishes, in order of priority, would you make to help us achieve our greatest potential?

The Micro-World Experience — Team Orienteering
During the first day, we introduced the group to the Continuous Learning Cycle, the AI 4-D Cycle, and their Affirmative Topic Statement (which had previously been crafted with the new company head). In order to augment the 4-D process, experiential

43

"solution-finding" initiatives with traditional AI Discovery and Dream interviews had been interspersed into the process. Throughout the afternoon, as an outcome of the exercises and interviews, the group continued to generate data around their peak leadership moments and their dreams for a collaborative leadership future. Before they left for the evening, they had prepared key provocative propositions to "live" in an experiential learning laboratory the next day.

Provocative Propositions

The leadership team's key provocative propositions included:

As leaders of our company, we provide our associates with the following:
- An environment that fosters open communication & facilitates and embraces change
- An atmosphere for total teamwork
- A commitment to common goals

We are compassionate and empathetic leaders that value and recognize the contributions of our associates.

We are proactive and make things happen.

We, as leaders, ask ourselves these questions every day:
- Am I living the vision & achieving goals that support that vision & our direction?
- Am I challenging myself to learn, grow & give my absolute best?
- Is my passion reaching other people?
- Am I asking "WHAT NEXT?"

Our vision statement comes alive through a proactive, results-oriented leadership team that is committed to building on the heritage that embodies our company.

Testing the Provocative Propositions

For the next afternoon session, we designed a complex orienteering course (outdoor navigation using map and compass skills) that the leadership team completed over a 3-hour period. To reflect the real-world fact that several team members worked remotely (at distant manufacturing plants), the team was divided into 2 sub-groups who communicated via walkie-talkies. Before starting the course, teams sent representatives to attend several seminars to learn new skills (map reading, compass use, pacing, strategy), which they then verbally transferred back to the other team members (reflecting Stephen Covey's 3-person teaching[8]). An Executive Edge facilitator accompanied each group throughout the orienteering course.

At each checkpoint, team members reviewed their provocative propositions in their Learning Journals and then faced a challenging "solution-finding" initiative (e.g. Group Juggle, Cup of Dreams, Process Control Review™ — see Sample Activity Descriptions below) that tested their ability to live the provocative propositions. After each challenge, the team debriefed the initiative, and shared their "best practices" with the other teams (via the walkie-talkies).

Throughout the orienteering course, the leadership team used the Continuous Learning Cycle as a guide for reflecting upon and analyzing each experience, and then strategizing for the next one. They found many opportunities to refine their provocative propositions, and even more significantly, they were able to experience a few peak moments as a highly functioning, cohesive team.

The design also offered strong metaphoric reflections of and connections to the workplace. At one of the checkpoints, a team member discovered that the other group had previously completed an initiative and chosen not to share its "best practices" with the rest of the leadership team. Rather intensely, he said, "This is exactly what I experience at work all of the time." As a remote plant manager, he felt out of the loop regarding key information, resources and decisions that had been made by other team members. The "real time" connection from the orienteering experience to the workplace allowed the group to see areas for growth as a leadership team, and to respond immediately.

45

Program Flow and Activity Sequence

The exercises and developed interview questions reflected issues like Shifting Leadership Paradigms (EL Exercise: Group Juggle to Warp Speed), Creating a Collective Vision (AI Interviews), Identifying & Prioritizing Core Values (EL Exercise: Cup of Dreams™), and Moving Dreams into Reality (EL Exercise: The Change Wave™). For example, in the classic experiential activity "Group Juggle to Warp Speed," the group must figure out how to juggle multiple objects (each person touching the objects in a repeatable sequence) as quickly as possible. In completing the task, they are challenged to look at their definition of "the possible" (is it one minute, 30 seconds or a seemingly impossible 2 seconds?) and get to experience how "out of the box" thinking leads to a shift in the group's perception.

In another activity, "Cup of Dreams," the group makes the connection between intentionally developed core values and achieving a shared vision. The group first identifies and then prioritizes the core values that drive their organization's vision. They then write those values on raw eggs that are balanced on a #10 tin can in the center of a large rope circle (that represents their "present state" as a group). Without stepping into the circle and using only the tools provided (bandana, some bungee cords, string and scissors), the group retrieves their core values from the present state and places them into "windows of opportunity" for the future. If any egg breaks, the group explores how the "lost core value(s)" might affect their vision. This discussion serves as an excellent point for further defining, articulating and understanding core values and group vision.

As outlined in the chart on page 47, these initial activities were woven into Discovery and Dream interviews and conversations, providing opportunities for increased rapport and empathy building within the group. During Design, trust-building opportunities developed as the team created, tested and refined its provocative propositions in the orienteering micro-world. And finally, conversations around defining, supporting and cascading out new principles of practice served to confirm a sense of mutual understanding among leadership team members.

Frontloading & Debrief Focus		Selected Structured Experiences with Continuous Learning Cycle Accelerate Relationships, Learning & Change
4- D Cycle	Relationship Continuum	
Discovery ===== Dream	Rapport ===== Empathy	• Appreciative Interviews • Group Juggle to Warp Speed • Cup of Dreams

Design	Trust	• Knowledge Sharing
		• Provacative Propositions
		• Team Orienteering
		  • Team Power Start™
		  • Learning the Ropes
		  • The Change Wave™ [9]

Destiny	Mutual Understanding	• Redefine Roots That Drive the Status Quo • Define Principles of Practice For Exemplary Leadership • Follow-up Sessions Cascade Principles of Practice & Relationship Building To Other Levels

Debriefing the Micro-World Experience

After the orienteering experience, the team returned to the classroom to discuss and condense the lessons they had learned and further define their principles of practice. They discussed the value that each team member brought to the leadership team, the impact that each member has on others and the way each person's work flows to others in their organization. Moreover, they prioritized and committed to a process for using new tools, making active changes within the group and "infecting others with our enthusiasm."

The leadership team was transformed at the end of the session. They had reinvented many aspects of their relationships and their community. Through their experience they redefined how they mutually understood terms such as: "exemplary leadership," "trust," "membership," "commitment," "representation," "teamwork," and "collaboration" in their company. As well, they outlined the initial steps for embracing a results-oriented, synergistic approach throughout the organization.

During the program, the leadership team experienced several real-time "peak moments" that illuminated their ideal collaborative future. They also had the opportunity to test and refine that affirmative future in a safe, non-threatening learning environment. As a result, they were able to design and commit to principles of practice that radically shifted their perceptions of their leadership roles within the organization.

The next chapter features another EL program that emphasizes the Destiny phase of an AI.

Project Success™
Participant-Generated Follow-up Correspondence

To: Project Success Participants

This package was prepared for you to share with the members of your staff or team. The contents include video highlights of the Project Success off-site team building event, briefing materials that include an overview of the event activities and guidelines for knowledge sharing, and the personal commitments you made during our follow-up meeting to share specific information and knowledge.

The next step: to bring the learned behaviors and concepts for strengthening and improving the working relationships between our groups back to our work environment where we will all continue to translate our shared vision into action.

There are 4 major outcomes/themes of our vision:
- Working Collaboratively and Linking Team Efforts
- Preplanning & Developing a Shared Vision
- Knowledge and Information Sharing
- Trust & Relationship Building

We encourage you to share these themes with your staff and/or team members and to actively apply the guiding principles of Project Success to your work environment. It is our hope that this package provides you with the tools to effectively share your experience and knowledge with the rest of your team.

It is critically important to our success that we continue the momentum by taking the next steps of Living our Vision ... Together.

Post-Program Follow-up Letter with
Video & Training Packet
For Project Success participants to cascade
throughout organization

6 Destiny
— Project Success, Bridging Silos

Chapter Six features the story of a Big Five Management Consulting firm's Finance and Information Technology Services divisions that merged to design and implement an Enterprise Resource Planning (ERP) software solution for the firm. The story illustrates the groups' experience with a "build-it yourself" High Ropes Challenge Course, and how they created follow-up to the program in order to generate critical mass for supporting change throughout their organization.

Benefits of Integration

Experiential Learning, when integrated into the Destiny (D^4) phase of an Appreciative Inquiry:

- Provides opportunities to create, experience, practice and refine provocative propositions and principles of practice — generating immediate feedback on their utility and effectiveness
- Creates learning environments to thaw and reshape communal understanding and behaviors
- Builds critical mass as change is cascaded throughout the community
- Helps the AI process kinesthetically "come alive" for all stakeholders

---

Situation Assessment

The Client Need

The Business, Engagement and Result Tracking (BERT) — enterprise-wide engagement tracking software — program was developed by the combined efforts of two divisions of a Big Five Management Consulting firm — Finance and Information Technology Services. BERT's scope covered engagement management systems, financial management systems and processes, along with the introduction of a new Information Warehouse (IW) and related access tools. Developing BERT involved coordinating hundreds of people in capturing business requirements, designing, building, testing, training and deploying new technology, processes and roles throughout the firm.

There were about 80 executives and managers representing the top of an organization that employed approximately 2,000 people. Most of the teams had been together for about three years, and, according to our clients (the Managing Partners of both divisions), they had been having some problems collaborating across formal and informal silos for the previous two years. While everyone was incredibly talented and committed, there was a fair amount of tension within the organization.

The clients related that the teams in both Divisions had developed a "tribal" loyalty (to their team) that superceded group or project loyalty. They felt that this dynamic was contributing to limited success on some major projects. The issue: the teams were not invested in achieving successful *group project outcomes*; rather their focus was mainly on *team success* on group projects. The attitude: "As long as my team comes through with a solution, it doesn't matter if the project fails as a result of another team's failure."

Additionally, they had approximately a dozen Subject Matter Experts (SMEs) who drove the silos and held the majority of the group's intellectual/knowledge capital. Most of the problem-solving was done in informal "hallway" meetings with one or a few SMEs. They viewed team-based or cross-team solution development as too cumbersome a process and avoided it. This contributed to the problem when other teams or individuals were needed,

52

and in most cases they didn't gain rapid support for their solution unless others were brought in from the beginning. It was difficult for them to understand that ultimately time and money would be saved if they started a project by engaging all stakeholders in the initial process, when everyone's skills, minds and innovations could work together to jointly develop a solution.

The executives managing these groups saw the need for developing a horizontal structure and horizontal processes that would eliminate, or at least bridge across, team and functional silos. As well, they believed that a hands-on, customized approach to learning would provide them with the fastest means for getting the lessons across, first to their managers, and then for building the momentum to drive the change out to other levels. At the end of this program the participants actually designed and built a physical model (a ropes course) of their horizontal structure, then climbed on it to complete project deliverables!

Building a collaborative team spirit was essential to this client's success. To be effective over time, team members needed to learn to collaborate both within work groups and between groups whose membership crossed departmental lines, jobs, roles, and subject matter expertise. This type of collaboration required trust, open channels of communication, appropriate business information, responsiveness to other's needs, and interpersonal competence.

Our goal was to help the team leaders (and by extension the teams) expand their thinking to encompass a more collaborative focus, to create unified solutions, and to think in terms of a "horizontal process" for underscoring and enabling a group-wide process orientation. As the client put it: "They (the team members) need to change their focus, to think in a bigger sense about the horizontal axis, the process axis, not the silo axis. To think in terms of We: How do we get out of this situation together? — vis-à-vis thinking in terms of Me: What can I do to get out of this situation? … People must understand how it has become one food chain — nobody stands alone any more."

The Micro-World Experience — Solution-Finding Initiatives and High Ropes Challenge

This integrated AI/EL program was a two-day design that metaphorically reflected real workplace circumstances and provided periods for group and individual reflection, experimentation and practice.

Initially it occurred to us that our client was trying to merge two distinctly different cultures — a Finance culture and a Technology culture working on a project requiring high levels of collaboration. Each group defined and approached certain aspects of community, like hierarchy and leadership, problem solving and decision-making, membership and representation, differently. Could it be that some of the tension might be a result of friction caused by these "style" differences?

As the program goals and the potential solutions developed, we suggested "style-switching" as one of the themes for the program. We felt that after observing, appreciating and even celebrating the groups' diversity, as reflected in the micro-world learning experience, the participants could predict where friction points would most likely occur (the points where interpersonal and intergroup tension is created) and develop group norms for reducing friction between groups. For this purpose, several weeks before the program, the participants completed a cultural orientation instrument (for indeed, Finance and Information Technology represented diverse internal cultures) that highlighted potential friction points in areas like time sensitivity and attention to hierarchy.

Program Flow and Activity Sequence

As with the other EL designs presented in this book, the program flow was based on the parallel processes outlined below:

Frontloading & Debrief Focus		Selected Structured Experiences with Continuous Learning Cycle Accelerate Relationships, Learning & Change
4 -D Cycle	Relationship Continuum	
Discovery Dream	Rapport ======= Empathy	• Pass the Zoop™ • Personal Power Walk • Obstacle Course/Balloon Castles Rotation • Team Islands • Paired & Group Appreciative Interviews
Design	Trust	• Create Provocative Propositions • Strategic Linking™/Trust V Rotation
Destiny	Mutual Understanding	• On Target Ropes Course • Action Planning • Team Leaders Cascade Project Success to All Levels • Quarterly Follow-Through

While the program flow followed the 4-D Cycle, the EL challenges illustrated the vertical and horizontal relationships, patterns and dynamics that existed among current relationships within the participant group. The participants had (and exercised) opportunities to transcend these patterns and work toward collaboration.

Day One Challenges

The challenges on Day One reflected the kinds of projects that the participants faced each day in their work.

Literally a vertical problem, "Balloon Castles" is visually and conceptually a silo challenge. With 100 balloons and two rolls of clear tape per team, teams are instructed to build the tallest free-standing, self-supporting balloon structure in a given time. Teams can choose whether to compete or collaborate (even though a competition is implied by the nature of the task) to make it a team or a group project. Balloon Castles illustrates how a vision at the beginning of a project may often result in a very different outcome.

When juxtaposed to Balloon Castles, the "Inflatable Obstacle Course" reflects a challenge that must be solved using a horizontally linked team process. It is a multi-team project that is successful when all teams contribute their deliverables to the project. The Obstacle Course illustrates how a project can break down when teams forge ahead on their own goals without regard for the goals, input and contributions of other teams on the project.

"Team Islands" is a challenge in which the group finds success by applying a horizontal process approach to a project. It addresses and illustrates the importance of developing "Horizontal Processes" while addressing an "Upstream Change and Accountability" issue for the Organization. Participants experience firsthand how "turfdom," established through exclusively defining roles and team boundaries, negatively affects group performance on a multi-team project.

In the afternoon of Day One, the participants debriefed Team Islands and the morning activities. This debrief tied the day together, building on the lessons from the morning while frontloading the next phase of the Appreciative Inquiry.

Once the physical challenges were finished for the day, the group reviewed the written responses from previous debrief sessions and interviews and began the process of creating provocative propositions. They derived the basis for their provocative propositions from the group strengths and successes they had discovered during the activities and the rapport, empathy, trust and mutual understanding that they had built during the day. They used the "Horizontal Structure" as a baseline upon which to extend their vision for the future. At the end of the first day the group had generated the following provocative propositions:

Project Success — Provocative Propositions

A shared vision is a clearly articulated statement of a desired future state. We believe that a shared vision, in order to be effective, must be:

- Well communicated
- Bought into with a feeling of ownership
- Visible commitment from above
- Tangible
- Achievable
- Meaningful
- Supporting overall mission

Having a shared vision is critical to the ultimate success of every initiative we undertake and therefore we will strive to always develop a shared vision.

1. We work collaboratively.
2. As citizens of the organization we have rights and responsibilities to obtain, build and share knowledge.
3. We proactively drive firm strategies in technology and finance.
4. We are operating under a COMMON VISION that is communicated clearly, and is understood by all. The vision is achievable through collaborative efforts that result in competitive advantage.
5. We operate and are recognized as a world-class, creative, value-adding organization.
6. We value and encourage each individual's contribution.
7. We attract, retain and challenge the best and brightest people.
8. We participate in a work environment that continually shares knowledge amongst its people.
9. We keep our people informed through honest, clear, timely and concise COMMUNICATIONS. These communications are tailored to the audience and delivered to appropriate levels of the organization!
10. We are the Global Glue: "Just Glue It!"
11. We are a world-class provider of financial and technical information services!

Day Two Challenges

On the morning of Day Two, the participants reviewed their provocative propositions with the intention of putting them to the test in a micro-world learning laboratory that reflected real world principles of their workplace.

Initially the teams rotated through two challenging activities — Strategic Linking™ and the Trust V — that raised the bar a bit on perceived physical risk-taking and interpersonal trust.

The "Strategic Linking" challenge (a 2" wide by 6" high by 50' long "circular" balance beam that must be simultaneously circumnavigated by multiple teams) encourages teams to explore the dynamic tensions that exist when linking teams on a project. Through examining their strengths in the context of the provocative propositions, they began operationalizing their horizontal structure.

The "Trust V" presents trust as a crucial element to successfully achieving the Horizontal Structure and provocative propositions. Beginning at the narrow end of a horizontal V (positioned 3 feet above the ground), partners hold hands and walk as far along their leg of the V as they possibly can. The rest of the group provides safety for the pair on the V by spotting for them and catching them when they fall off. Each of these activities also included affirmative front-loading and debriefing. As well, the group continued to look at their provocative propositions in the context of the challenges, their work and the horizontal structure.

After lunch and a short stretch, the teams entered the "Hockey Arena" where they discovered a 50 foot high scaffolding structure custom-made for Project Success: On Target™. In this culminating challenge, teams literally design and build a physical model of a horizontal structure, while developing a horizontal process for communicating and working together.

During this "build-it yourself high ropes challenge" teams are challenged to deliver their subject matter expertise from separate silos (portable pamper poles 16 feet high) to targets situated around a 50 foot square, without touching the ground outside of their perimeter (located at each corner of the structure). With the provocative propositions to guide their horizontal process the participants

58

literally created vertical silos, and then built bridges between the silos in order to achieve their goals — creating and utilizing a physical model of the horizontal structure.

Using the horizontal structure that they had created, teams delivered their subject matter expertise to the designated targets. Of course, they found it necessary to re-start several times as they realized the challenges involved with adopting a horizontal process.

This challenge reflects a multi-team project in which success is achieved only when teams collaborate with each other to reach a common goal. It tied both days together and prepared the group for the final Design and Destiny session called "The Horizontal Structure at Work."

Debriefing the Micro-World Experience — The Horizontal Structure at Work

In this final session, the leaders of the FI&TS group co-developed plans for bringing their provocative propositions to life and cascading them throughout their workplace. Specifically, they responded to the following:

1. Identify the provocative proposition that will best support relationship building at work.
2. Develop a plan that will best communicate your commitment to the future.

The next step was to bring the learned behaviors and concepts for strengthening and improving working relationships between the groups back to work where they would all continue to translate their shared vision into action. Ultimately they identified four key outcomes of their vision that would re-write the rules for who they are and would redefine the relationships between the two groups based on what they had just experienced together:

- Working Collaboratively and Linking Team Efforts
- Preplanning & Developing a Shared Vision
- Knowledge and Information Sharing
- Trust & Relationship Building

Initially they shared these themes with staff and team members and actively applied the guiding principles of Project Success to their work environment. While this is impressive in and of itself for a two-day experience, they went further.

The Hand-Off

One of the best ways to gauge the success of an AI is to assess how well an organization continues on toward achieving its destiny after the consultant leaves. In the case of FI&TS this hand-off went extremely well. With minimal post-session shadow consulting over the next 12 months, the groups continued to focus on their collaborative process with two follow-up sessions called "We've Got to Live It Together" and "Living It Together."

These sessions were also EL-based and they further developed the concepts from Project Success. One of these sessions involved creating videos that effectively communicated the vision to the divisions' managers and staff, while further strengthening relationships and reinforcing alignment and commitment to the vision. The sessions also helped renew each person's commitment to the guiding principles, while providing tools for more easily and effectively cascading them out to the rest of the organization.

One year later, our clients felt that they had made such great progress that they were ready to shift their OD efforts from focusing on building horizontal relationships and processes to developing individual management competencies. To date, they continue rolling out this process.

7 Self-Facilitated Team Learning

Reinventing Experiential Learning and Redefining The Facilitator's Role

As a result of discovering and implementing the insights presented below, we have reinvented EL for ourselves and our clients, and have redefined the role of the experiential facilitator in our practice.

Insight One: Focus on the Learning Objectives First, Then Choose the Experience

EL is more than adventure challenges, games or other "team building activities." When EL is at its best, the choice of venue is driven by the learning objectives for the program. As experiential educators, when we truly give integrity to our work, we understand that the design of the overall program flow is driven by the learning objectives, rather than the experiences themselves. This insight caused us to make a profound shift in our thinking about EL, changing from an "activity focus" (the means) to a "learning focus" (the end). As a result, a whole new world of experiences opened up: classroom and computer simulations, community service, creative arts (music, theater, improvisation, dance, video production), and fine arts, to name a few.

Insight Two: Focus on Self-Facilitation

Since the early 1990's, we have been integrating a Self-Facilitated Team Learning approach into virtually all of our EL program designs. As previously mentioned in this book, the self-facilitated aspect creates a learner-centered focus that we have found to be far more effective, and result in greater value for our clients than many facilitator-led EL designs.

Traditionally speaking, Appreciative Inquiry is a self-facilitated learning process. While interview scripts guide the direction of discovery and dreaming, people conduct the interviews without a facilitator to lead them. They also work fairly independently when creating provocative propositions and designing principles of practice for their organization. Indeed, the focus of the AI facilitator is to rapidly hand off the learning process to the people who are discovering, dreaming, designing and living their destiny together.

As well, scripting interviews, and designing summits to be self-led makes sense from an AI outcome perspective. Accuracy and comprehensiveness in the data collection process can impact the outcome of an AI process tremendously. The more dependent a process is on a facilitator's interpretation of the material, outcomes, questions, etc. the more widely the collected data will potentially vary. Self-facilitated learning experiences provide the potential for much more accurate and complete data collection, by creating a standardized experience across the whole group.

The Facilitator's Role

In evolving toward a self-facilitated learning approach, we have come to believe that in order for EL practitioners to successfully integrate AI they need to reevaluate how they define the role of the facilitator and the way in which they design programs. For example, one goal of an experiential "team building" session is to accelerate a team's process of moving through fairly predictable stages of team development. We began observing that facilitator-led teams tended to stall at certain stages and were not able to move forward to the next developmental stages. For instance, rather than working through their own internal "storming" process, they would "storm" at the facilitator — "You didn't mention that rule," "We didn't think that was enough of a touch," etc. They escaped dealing with their own internal storming (and consequently moving forward in their team development) through the mechanism of storming at the facilitator.

Moreover, in facilitator-led sessions the participants continually watch the facilitator for "hints" or "signals" as to how next to proceed. Typically, the facilitator introduces and frontloads the activity, "polices" the activity (enforces the consequences of breaching the rules of the activity) and debriefs the activity — all the while attempting to be ghost-like and not remain the central focus of the group. Yet, in facilitator-led sessions, the facilitator *always* has the focus of the group. This kind of approach reflects the familiar, or typical sort of Experiential Learning program that many of us have either experienced or led. It is familiar to us because it is widely practiced, primarily because it is a very effective means for delivering experiential learning. Yet, this dynamic reflects a rather schizophrenic relationship of "dependence versus independence" with regard to the facilitator.

In a self-facilitated learning approach, the Learning Journal guides the process while placing the learning almost entirely into the hands of the participants. This approach is especially effective in compressed time situations (in which learning cycle times are drastically cut) with large groups of people, such as in an AI change process. The Learning Journal contains everything that the participants need to create their own story and facilitate their own learning processes — activity frontloading, scenario, rules and reflective debrief questions which comprise both scaling questions and open-ended narrative type questions.

Participants who are self-facilitating manage their own time, call their own process breaks, prioritize the value of doing (or not doing) each activity, and conduct their own debriefs. They learn how to facilitate a process for extracting meaningful learning from experience while reaching toward the goal of continuous improvement — They move from dependence to independence from an external facilitator, and through self-facilitation they develop a spirit of interdependence within their team or participant group. The facilitator is thus freed to elevate learning to another level.

63

Standardized Experiences

Standardization of the experience is another important reason for adopting a self-facilitated learning approach. While this approach is effective with any size group, it is especially effective in large group situations wherein it is important that individuals and groups have similar experiences, as in an AI. One critical outcome of the Discovery and Dream phases of the 4-D Cycle is data collection. While the data collected during these phases is qualitative, or colloquial, it is important that the collection process is consistent. This is why, in AI, an interview protocol is developed for the interviewers to use with interviewees. The interview protocol usually includes interview tips, an introduction and interview questions. The interviewer is asked to stay as much as possible within the guidelines of the interview protocol, asking the questions as they are specifically worded, while encouraging the interviewee to speak openly and freely in their response to the questions.

In contrast, many EL programs employ what we call a "Facilitator in a bag" approach. Simply put, several facilitators (one for each team of participants) travel to the site, usually arriving the day before the program. Each facilitator brings their own duffle bag containing their own personal favorite activities. The EL company providing the program conducts a briefing for the facilitators, describing the client's rationale for doing the program, the history leading up to the program and the client's learning objectives. They also cover any logistical concerns in the few hours slated for facilitator orientation. That evening the facilitators, either independently or in groups, and relying on the activities that they brought with them in their duffle bag, create their design. The outcome is that each team's experience varies widely. Not only do the activities differ, but activity frontloading and debrief questions presented by the facilitator (and, therefore, the answers the participants provide) vary as well.

Even when the activities are carefully selected by the EL provider to fit their client's learning objectives, without a carefully designed Learning Journal (providing activity frontloading, rules and debrief questions) each team's experience varies greatly. This is because, in a facilitator-led approach, each minute of the experience is subject to a wide variety of interpretations depending on the facilitator.

Artfully designed self-facilitated learning programs are not subject to such widely diverse experiences, and therefore, the data collected for the ongoing AI process much more accurately reflects the overall group standard.

One final clarifying point about self-facilitated learning experiences: Self-facilitated learning experiences are open-ended and they are not. Since the hope is to gain specific objectives and targeted outcomes, the process and people are guided toward those objectives and outcomes — very much like a highway that provides lanes, signs and exit ramps in order to guide people to safely and efficiently reach their destinations. At the same time, the process is open-ended, "destinations" (desired objectives and outcomes) are suggested and defined by the choice of "lanes," however, the participants co-create their own "milestones" equating to insights, solutions, strategies and so on toward generating a communal future. The process is as open-ended and as structured, no more and no less, as a traditional AI.

Understanding and implementing these insights into application and practice is a critical step toward developing the capacity to integrate AI with EL.

8 The Beginning

Organizations today require the capacity to change rapidly, so in this respect learning and change cycle times have become just as important as product cycle times. As important as this fact is, organizations of any size have difficulty gaining the traction necessary for achieving rapid, sustainable and systemic change. Appreciative Inquiry (AI), through storytelling, provides a solution to this dilemma and in the preceding chapters we have suggested a means for augmenting, deepening and accelerating the AI process by integrating Experiential Learning (EL).

In considering the potential for integrating the two approaches it is important to keep in mind the basis for AI: the Five Principles of Appreciative Inquiry. When integrating any approach with AI, the approach should resonate with and support these Five Principles. One should be able to demonstrate how the added approach creates a synergistic whole that is coherent with, and supportive of, the five principles, rather than just accessorizing for the sake of adding another approach.

The Five Principles of AI and How EL Supports Them

Principle #1: The Constructionist Principle

The first principle of AI, the Constructionist Principle, essentially maintains that knowing and destiny are interwoven — Organizations are living, human constructions whose fate is a reflection and extension of the communal knowledge that created them. Human beings and organizations move in the direction that their knowledge and inquiries take them. It's not "what" you know, but "how" you know.

Through practicing AI we hope to create a more intentional "knowing" that helps to guide an organization toward a deliberately chosen, and affirmative destiny.

This is one of the most difficult concepts to convey in an AI. Most people don't believe that they create their own workplace realities. And, as Peter Senge mentions in his book *The Fifth Discipline*, in many organizations the belief that "we can't create our own futures" is so great that it eludes acknowledgement[10]. Under these circumstances people don't have the experience that their contributions create their current realities. Therefore, they don't see how they could possibly contribute to changing their reality, no less how they might intentionally create their own future.

EL micro-worlds provide opportunities for creating a different kind of "knowing" for all stakeholders. They are places where certain kinds of experiments can be tried that could never be attempted in real work settings. In EL micro-worlds, individual contributions to current realities are obvious and even small changes create dramatic shifts in the potential future. Over the course of a few short hours, a group of people who are immersed in an integrated AI/EL micro-world create their own "intentional mini-society" that is a reflection of the ideal future. The relationships between "how people know" and their "destiny" are illustrated for every person who experiences an EL micro-world.

Through EL people experience their organization as a living expression of themselves. They gain confidence in the belief that they can shape their future through intentionally changing their current reality.

Principle #2: The Principle of Simultaneity

The Principle of Simultaneity (AI Principle #2) holds forth that inquiry and change, rather than being separate moments, happen simultaneously. The seeds of change are sown by the first questions that we ask and, therefore, the future that we reap is the product of the approach that we use when beginning to inquire about change. As in a quantum leap, where an atom doesn't exist until we look for it, and then it instantaneously appears wherever we look for it, the questions that we ask create the foundation for what we "discover" which then becomes the basis for conceiving and building the future.

In an integrated AI/EL micro-world, participants don't have to just accept this principle as fact, they can actually *experience* inquiry and intervention as one simultaneous event. They can observe and understand how inquiry and intervention are inextricably related to defining existing and new realities — Due to the compressed time nature of the micro-world environment, any inquiry results in an almost immediate impact on the group's current and future realities.

Moreover, it is widely accepted that the best time to observe a situation, whether a problem or a solution, is at the precise moment when it happens. To "predict" a circumstance before it happens creates the potential for developing inaccurate assumptions. To "recall" a situation after the fact is to potentially miss any number of salient points that may be essential to understanding what created the circumstance. As well, due to the complexities of the workplace it is difficult, if not impossible, to observe many circumstances, no less to understand their cause and effect on current or future realities.

In an EL micro-world the complexities of the workplace are stripped away and the group is left with the basic, or foundational relationships that created the current organization (for better or worse). Here not only is the inquiry/intervention placed into the moment, but causal relationships are also readily apparent. The status quo, here expressed as patterns and dynamics that reflect workplace realities, is illustrated as if it were highlighted on a relief map of the organization. Active experimentation at this point

69

enables an organization to test any number of responses, thus illustrating and clarifying which response may likely lead to reaching the most desired future.

Principle #3: The Poetic Principle

The Poetic Principle (Principle #3) implies that an organization's "story" can be rewritten at any time. While the organization's story is constantly being co-authored, its past, present or future are an endless source for interpretation, inspiration, or learning. What this principle implies is that any number of current or new realities can flow from a simple reinterpretation of the organization's story, just as there may be numerous potential interpretations for any given poem. AI, through its affirmative orientation, helps to create confirmatory interpretations of virtually any exploration into a human system or organization.

EL augments and supports this aspect of AI by bringing out the best of people and organizations through the interactions that happen in the micro-world. Furthermore, the Continuous Learning Cycle outlines a step-by-step process for guiding a group's exploration of the "best of what exists" and the "best of what could be." Beginning with affirmatively frontloading and then confronting a structured experience, the group reflects on factual accounts of the experience discovering best practices, patterns and dynamics that support success. Based on their experience they also develop and then experiment with real-world principles that enable the group to move in the direction of the new, desired future. As they create their new future, they build interpersonal relationships that are essential to encouraging the ongoing dialogue necessary to giving life to and sustaining the future.

Principle #4: The Anticipatory Principle

One of the pillars of AI is the notion of the vision, or image of the future, as the guiding force behind current behavior of the organization. The Anticipatory Principle (AI Principle #4) holds forth that the most important resource for generating constructive organizational change is the communal imagination and dialogue about the future. Organizations exist because the people who guide and keep the organization on track share a mutual understanding about the organization's purpose, how it functions and what it will become.

According to Peter Senge " ... a vision can die if people forget their connection to one another."[11] Without deep interpersonal connections maintained by regular dialogue, a carefully crafted communal vision rapidly becomes the "official" vision. The result is a vision that is proselytized but which is not truly believed in or understood by all, thus creating divisiveness in the organization with insiders and outsiders to the vision.

An integrated AI/EL approach as we have described in the preceding chapters solidifies interpersonal relationships and encourages in-depth dialogue about many aspects of current and future realities. It intentionally pursues building relationships through creating and enhancing rapport, empathy and trust out of which flows mutual understanding.

Furthermore, implied in the Anticipatory Principle is the notion that in order for AI to come alive in an organization, people need to believe in, and have confidence in, their ability to impact their current and future realities. The force that ultimately gives life to an organization is the people's understanding of the vision and their confidence in their ability to influence their reality in order to continually create and work toward achieving their vision.

Principle #5: The Positive Principle

Finally, the Positive Principle (AI Principle #5) is the result of years of experience observing how positive affect and social bonding influence long-term change. Experience with AI tells us that the more positive questions posed when community building, the more effective and long lasting the change.[12] As Principle #1 states, humans and the organizations that we create gravitate toward the direction that we inquire. Affirmatively oriented interviews with thousands of people will have an entirely different long-term impact on sustained positive action than will studying organizational "problems" or "issues."

By extension, EL provides opportunities for organizational "peak experiences," short periods when everyone feels "aligned" and moving toward the same shared objective. These moments are

71

"addictive." Once they have experienced a moment like this, people make every attempt to recreate the circumstances around which it occurred. Micro-world based peak experiences provide positive momentum and group alignment toward a communal destiny. By experiencing these moments together, people develop a synergy that resonates with and focuses their energy toward a shared objective. This energy becomes coherent, and like the light from a laser, it vibrates and builds on itself continually generating new capacities, opportunities and achievements.

In general, when immersed in an affirmative micro-world, group members gain insight into individual and team behaviors, attitudes and strategies that contribute to effectiveness that are often reflected in the form of interpersonal relationships, patterns and dynamics. They then develop and practice strategies for improvement. This safe and challenging environment is designed to be highly interactive, dynamic, engaging and reflective so that it triggers spontaneous responses from the team members that accurately mirror their workplace behaviors, patterns and dynamics back to them. In our case we provide self-guided opportunities for reflective learning within the micro-world experience that we call "Self-Facilitated Team Learning."

Since structured experiences are designed to be challenging but have "neutral" outcomes, both negative consequences and positive benefits of strategies and interpersonal interactions occur. Guided reflection enables participants to strategize, practice and gain confidence in new skills and insights, personal styles and behaviors that have a positive impact on individual, team and/or organizational performance. Since learning and change cycle times are as important to our clients as are product cycle times, this accelerated approach to learning and change provides incredible value for them. This brand of EL is particularly effective in cases wherein content cannot be taught, but it can be learned, as in learning leadership or teamwork.

It is our hope that you will see that Experiential Learning contributes to (1) the flow toward mutual understanding that is required in order for community members to support the future and

72

live their integrity and destiny, (2) accelerating and deepening the rapport of the participants, and (3) strengthening the experience of honest communal vision that is deeply understood and enlivened. Please continue the conversation.

Glossary of Terms & Definitions

Affirmative Topic Statement — A bold, assertive and positively-crafted statement (or set of statements) that reflects the topic choice for an Appreciative Inquiry.

Appreciative Inquiry — An affirmative philosophy, process and approach to finding and co-creating a new, more positive future for a person, group, organization, or community.

Continuous Learning Cycle™ — An action - reflection model for extracting meaningful learning from experiences and applying new insights to improving performance.

Experiential Initiatives — Mental and/or physical challenges designed to reflect real life circumstances with the intent of catalyzing purposeful learning. Of short duration, several of these challenges together may constitute a micro-world.

Experiential Learning — A process for achieving personal or communal growth and development as a result of gaining insights through guided experiencing, reflecting and acting.

Frontloading — A "framing statement" describing the real life case for an experiential initiative that bridges the metaphoric gap between reality and the micro-world learning environment.

Micro-world experience — "These are microcosms of real business settings where teams of managers learn together by conducting experiments that are difficult or impossible to conduct in real business. Developing a micro-world involves research to understand the systemic structures underlying particular business issues, then develop a learning process for managers who work and live with these issues day by day."
Peter Senge, *The Fifth Discipline*, pg. 299

Principles of Practice — Working agreements that are based on provocative propositions and an articulated positive core. Make reinventing the present (and therefore the future) possible.

Provocative Proposition — Statement that describes a new future, challenges the status quo, inspires action and is worded in the present tense as if it were the current reality.

Relationship Continuum™ — Predictable stages in a group or team's progression toward achieving trust and mutual understanding. Beginning with building rapport and developing empathy, a group intentionally creates an environment in which trust can be established and nurtured. Once trust is established, mutual understanding is possible.

Self-facilitated Learning™ — A learner-centered process for extracting meaningful, targeted learning from experiences wherein learners explore new insights with minimal external guidance.

Self-facilitated Team Learning™ — A learner-centered process for extracting meaningful, targeted *team* learning from experiences wherein learners explore new insights with minimal external guidance.

Team Learning Journal™ — A manual for guiding self-facilitated (team) learning in micro-world environments.

Endnotes

1. Throughout this book, we define community in an organizational context. Workplace community is defined as:

   " ... an organization that is interconnected, productive and beneficial. It is integrative and inclusive. People work well together because they are interdependent *and* autonomous. Together they create an atmosphere where members want to contribute with high levels of responsibility, activities of partnering and collaboration. The goal is to impact the survival and growth of the members and the overall organization." Per conversation with Jane Seiling, September 10, 2001.

2. Kolb, David (1982). *Experiential Learning: Experience as the Source of Learning and Development.* Englewood Cliffs, NJ: Prentice Hall.

3. Our thanks to Dr. Robert Means of the Veteran's Administration for sharing the Three C's with us.

4. Similar to the micro-worlds described by Peter Senge in *The Fifth Discipline* (1990). New York, NY: Doubleday.

5. Cooperrider, David L. and Diana Whitney (1998). *Appreciative Inquiry: A Constructive Approach to Organization Development and Social Change.* Workshop manual presented through the Dively Center for Management Development, Case Western Reserve University.

6. Hargrove, Robert (1998). *Mastering the Art of Creative Collaboration.* New York, NY: McGraw Hill, 12.

7. Whitney, Diana and David L. Cooperrider (2000). The Appreciative Inquiry Summit: An Emerging Methodology for Whole System Positive Change. *OD Practitioner.* 13-26.

8. Covey, Steven R. (1989). *Seven Habits of Highly Effective People*. New York: NY: Fireside.

9. The Change Wave™ name, scenario, frontloading and rules were originally written and copyrighted by Executive Edge, Inc. in 1994.

10. Senge, Peter (1990). *The Fifth Discipline*. New York, NY: Doubleday. 231.

11. Senge, Peter (1990). *The Fifth Discipline*. New York, NY: Doubleday. 230.

12. Busche, G. and G. Coetzer (March 1995). Appreciative Inquiry as a Team-Development Intervention: A Controlled Experiment. *Journal of Applied Behavioral Science*. 13.

TO ORDER FOCUS BOOKS

Web: www.taosinstitute.net

Phone: 888/999-TAOS
or 440/338-8308

Fax: 440/339-5713

Mail: Taos Institute Publications
c/o Executive Edge Inc.
46 Chagrin Plaza #147
Chagrin Falls, OH 44022

Shipping Address

Name _____
Title _____
Company _____
Address _____
City _____
State _____ Zip _____
Country _____
Phone _____ Fax _____
Email _____

Quantity	Book Title	Price	Total
	ISBN: 0-9712312-2-2 *Experience AI: A Practitioner's Guide to Integrating AI with Experiential Learning*	$14.95	
		Tax	
		Shipping	
		Total	

Shipping and Handling

Total Order	Rate
$0.00 — $20.00	$5.25
$20.0 — $50.00	$5.50
Over $50.00	11 % of total

Ohio residents add 6% sales tax.

All orders within continental U.S. are shipped via UPS Ground, but express delivery is available. Contact Customer Service Department for Express Delivery options and rates, or for shipping charges on bulk orders.

Outside Continental U.S. All orders are shipped as educational materials. Express Delivery and any customs/ duties are the buyer's responsibility.

All prices are in U.S. dollars, and are subject to change without notice.